THE MUSIC OF THE OCEAN

David Hodges

The Music of the Ocean

© David Hodges 2013

ISBN 9780956688415
Acknowledgements
Spirituality, Religious life Review,
The Merton Journal and **The Merton Seasonal**
in which some of these poems first appeared

Published by The Abbey, Caldey Island,
Tenby, Pembs. SA70 7UH, Wales, G.B.

The Music of the Ocean

The Music of the Ocean

The music of the ocean brings
awareness of another journey
I must make,
a hunger not yet fed.
The heart must have its way:
it knows where and what it seeks
in the salt sea breeze,
in the rhythm of the waves.
It is for the heart alone
to question why,
in silence hear the answer—
or continue in a life less free.

Hope

The howling wind,
the rain and driving sand,
all painted cold and grey;
and then a shaft of light,
a clearing sky,
a rainbow meets the sea,
the starlings play in flight.

Trees begin to bud,
the marram sprouts,
no need to doubt
that Spring will come,
all signs of hope,
impatient for
the coming of the sun.

The Moods of the Sea

What does the sea feel?
Let's colour in all its moods
from leaden grey to icy blue,
from oily black to tropical green;
from all that's been seen

of its heart and its soul,
to distress or console,
in its gentle calm,
or wildly out of control
in all its sound and its fury.

What can we hear in its voice,
in the crash of the waves,
in the spume and the spray,
or in the calm where dolphins play?
Does it wonder at being alive?

What can we see in the face of the sea
when it's clear and still like glass,
or full of passionate appeal?
What does it sense and feel,
from the cold of the poles

to the heat of the tropics,
from coconut to halibut,
from the sweet scent of the palm
to the stench of rotting fish?
Does it hope or wish?

In the Ebb and Flow

In the ebb and flow,
in the flotsam, the jetsam,
the driftwood of a life—
its occasional treasure.
But now that I have ceased
to search for
the perfect stone or shell,
all is gift,
all is surprise,
all in its proper light.

In the ebb and flow,
a letting go.
After winter's storms,
the warmth
of the sun's caress,
the kiss of gentle waves,
days of joy and stillness,
all forgiven, now at peace,
waiting, listening,
hoping.

The Sandpiper

All day
grim and grey.
White of gull and foam
dance against the monochrome.
A sandpiper pecking
even as the sun is setting,
focused on the strand,
its whole world absorbed in sand;
unaware of the ocean,
or the commotion
of gulls in flight
before the fading of the light.

High Cliff Quarry

An ugly gap remains,
a scarred and empty place
still slowly healing
from a brutal commerce.
Empty now of man-made noise,
home to lesser black-backs,
herring-gulls and fulmars.
A fragment of a jetty,
where perhaps the ketches
or the barges moored, that left
to go as far as Bristol,
loaded down with limestone blocks
for merchants' sea-front mansions;
fine Welsh stone now fouled
by some foreign gull or pigeon.

A deserted space,
unnaturally cut,
its steep height impresses;
now not much disturbed,
as if the present silence
had been quarried out
to leave it softly greening over.
Now resting from discordant sounds
of the blast, the pick,
the saw and the hammer;
from the noise of the hewing, splitting,
cutting and the shaping.
Now allowing just the cry
of nesting gulls,
the soothing symphony
of the sea.

Nothing in November

November's not a good time.
Don't ask me when's a good time—
but November's not a good time
to leave the island
to get that back tooth seen to,
to catch the Eurostar to Belgium,
or to get that double hernia repaired.
No, November's not a good time
to get that sofa over,
to send the cattle off for slaughter,
or to get that new electric cable
laid beneath the sea.
I can't think when's a good time—
but November's not a good time
for anything but staying put.
No, November's not a good time
to rely on the wind dropping
and the mail boat crossing,
to get you to and from the island.
No, November's really not a good time.
There'll be nothing in November.

Tenby Harbour

The little harbour silent
in the faintly growing light;
the dark band of the harbour wall,
tall houses by the water's edge.

The salt air, the harbour smells,
the first gull's cry;
the moon still high and watching
for the tidal rush and swirl.

Roped and chained to moorings,
boats sheltered by the quay
begin a slow dance on the water,
glad to be freed by the sea's return.

Nature's surge of joy delights,
restless beauty now unfolding,
grace-filled rhythms surprised
by the sight of each new day.

Crossing from Tenby

White roads hugging
bays and rocky cliffs,
threading tiny farms
to cottages and hamlets.
Then a church and castle ruin,
small villages,
the railway crossing.

The town laid out
in not quite geometric streets,
narrow connecting alleys
unchanged since Tudor times.
Old town walls, St Mary's Church,
Victorian houses now hotels,
the Tudor Merchant's House,

St Julian's Chapel,
the harbour noise, the smell of fish.
Bells ring out across the waves,
the sound of boats,
the lapping water.
Soon the tide is full;
our boat makes distance
from the harbour quay.

A Day at Tautra Mariakloster*

The Church all wood and glass,
lit up like a lighthouse
in our Vigil prayer,
rising in the dark night air
for those in sorrow or despair.

By the old grey boathouse,
mist and rain disperse.
Seabirds on the shoreline;
the sun begins to shine
on gulls and terns

awake since early nocturns.
Water lapping gently,
sanderlings intently
studying the tidal menu.
Sky and fjord, blue on blue.

Bright, late morning,
warming sun.
Oystercatchers joining,
amid the stones and muck,
the snipe and eiderduck.

After Sext and None,
afternoon draws on;
blossom on plum and pear,
the warm air, and not a sound
until the Vespers bell resounds.

At Compline, through our wall of glass,
pure chance, entranced,
we see a newbuilt oil rig pass,
towed slowly up the fjord,
as we praise and bless Our Lord.

*Cistercian monastery of nuns
on the Trondheim fjord of Norway

Vigils

'To him belongs the sea for he made it
and the dry land shaped by his hands'.
Vigils! And the storm lifts the roofboards
as we intone psalm ninety-four,
to the howl and whistle of the wind
and the sea's roar on the nearby shore,
to the scattering rain
against the window pane.

His will to test and shape us
as we struggle harder
with our chant and prayer
for this his troubled world
and his creation,
held in his love and care,
in this dark crucible
amid the storm before the dawn.

Night Watchmen

The lighthouse keeper,
in his hours of watch,
his solitary ministry
to ships in danger,
to all in peril on the sea,
waiting for the beam of light
that sweeps across the night
to fade to morning light.
A ritual marking
of the hours of darkness,
giving warning,
guiding and protecting.

The hermit monk at prayer,
at his lonely vigil
on the night watch.
Beacon of love,
in darkness bringing light,
praying for all in peril
in the terror of the night.
His priestly ministry
to watch and wait
seven times a day,
in trust and faith
that prayer is valid.

A Day in the Life of a Monk

'How many years…?'
the stranger asks.
I no longer know,
I have no guide;
the present seems to fill
all time, prayer fills
all the spaces.

The day moves on
from psalm to psalm,
the Abbey bell records
the passing years
on my island home.

Lavender blooms and fades,
the sun is high or low,
the swallows come and go,
the graveyard fills
with wooden crosses;
still the same
white cowls in choir.

Yet, stranger, tell me
if my place is filled.
Tell me, is my psalter spread,
or am I there
among the dead?

Swallows

There is a hush before they rise.
I sense it is their final flight,
joyful as they leave,
bound for a brighter place
as the days begin to fade.
They have been preparing long,
the wires now bare
between the lighthouse and the farm.

The coffin bearers pause
before the rush of wings
that fills the eastern sky.
They're up upon their way
as we mourn and pray
to celebrate the mystery
of this passage
to new life.

Sand Dunes

Far from the crowd
bright sun appeared through cloud;
time scarcely seemed to pass,
looking lazily through the marram grass,
lying high up in the sand
as people passed, repassed, along the strand.

Thoughts then passed to prayer
in the warm and sultry air;
and all my past I recalled, forgave,
lost in the gently lapping waves.
Boats lay off, the sea was calm,
all thoughts suspended, nature's balm.

The Sand Garden

A grassy bank,
an old iron tank,
sundial, paths
and stepping stones;
atop the sand
a red watering can,
a rake and spade.

Bay trees shade
sorrel and sweet cicely,
chervil, chives and comfrey;
next a box cross,
oxlip, viper's bugloss.
Then come silver, greys and blues,
yarrow, tarragon and rue,

french thyme and southernwood,
dill and catmint, wormwood.
Hot and dry, wide open to the sky,
lavender in full sun,
rosemary, sage, verbascum,
love-in-the-mist and liquorice,
ginger mint, pinks, horseradish.

Butterflies, moths and bees,
insects in dry leaves.
A wagtail struts;
a lazy cat, eyes half shut,
puts an end
to thoughts of Zen.

The Old Apple Orchard

Old Father Désiré,
I remember brandishing
his stick aloft,
charging down the garden
at full tilt,
lapsing into Belgian French
at the harsh pruning
of his beloved trees.
Beauty of Bath, Duke of Devonshire,
Early Worcester, Winston, Epicure...
old varieties now out of favour.

His beloved trees
now badly overgrown,
each variety once mapped
and marked and listed
according to its orchard.
The old apple shed in ruins,
overrun with rats,
where once were row on row
of labelled crates
and wooden slatted boxes,
full of apples wrapped and stored.

I remember his delight at sampling
the first of each new crop:
'Ah, Beauty of Bath…'
Like a taster of fine wines,
he knew each one,
how long to lay them down,
what month to eat them;
all carefully noted
in his little book, now lost.
Would he eat or spurn
our modern crop of Braeburns?

Catching God at Work*

Is He
in the lacing tracery
of the branches of
the wind-torn trees?

Is He
in the cloud-masked light
of the early morning's
watery sun?

Is He
high up unseen there
with the ecstatic
music of the lark?

Is He
there with young love,
wild and feral,
fire in the blood?

Is He
there beyond the setting sun,
beyond the ocean's rim?

Is He
in the first footprints
on the virgin snow?

Is He
in the wild places,
in the spaces in the wildwood,
where no word is heard?

Is He
there in the daily
question-raising mystery
at the heart of all our lives?

Is He
there in the silence
of this sacred space
between the candle and the dark?

*Einstein said he had 'spent (his) whole
life trying to catch God at his work'.

Transforming Silence

In the desert of the night,
before the dawn, in faith
beyond all pain and darkness,
to wait to be enfolded
by a silence so complete,
to penetrate so deep,
to feel his presence
somewhere far within.
Filled with his love,
the prayer of Jesus' name
now breaks upon the stillness
of this conscious space.

Emmaus

Will you find Him
on the way?
Someone like you but more
yourself than yourself,
your heart's truth.

Feeling His presence,
all that you desire,
opening to Him,
freeing you to love,
with His love

flowing through you
to the other;
your heart aflame
to love and to be loved,
loved into the One.

Eucharist

His word spoken,
love awoken in all hearts,
his Father's love
that he imparts,
that we might love
like him, poured out
the world throughout.

Christ came to serve,
chosen, blessed,
his body broken
and the pieces shared,
that we might be his body
and be one,
living for each other.

To go beyond
the word we heard,
to serve, to love
as he loved us,
to be one, one spirit,
as the Father and the Son
are One.

The Station Mass*

Quarry tiles and copper pots and pans,
cabbage smells and hanging hams,
kitchen chairs, old oak table, the priest's soutane.
We in our Sunday best, all spick-and-span,
solemnly breaking bread, recalling, we believe,
life given that we may receive.
Around the kitchen table, love released;
Eucharist becomes agape feast.
Now we seem able,
at the kitchen table,
to act more tolerantly,
to look at someone differently.
Not letting virtue displace—
or get in the way of—grace.
Seeing in each one something
loveable and loving;
original beauty we recall, reteach;
others heal and mend a breach.
All now sharing, gratefully accepting;
all differences forgetting .

Irish house Mass

No, They Were Never Satisfied

No, they were never satisfied,
those great men
whose names live on.
No, they never, none of them,
fully realised their dream.
We have their works—
to them they gave
no lasting pleasure.

The creative urge,
the climax at completion,
then the niggling doubt,
the dwelling on past failure,
the fault that only they could see.
The need, the absolute need,
to bring to birth again.
That painful, arid gap.

Those great men
never rested on their laurels,
the adulation of other men.
But does God perhaps demand
it of them, that they put
this drive aside?
Perhaps it conflicts
with selfless love of God?

Or does He perhaps demand
that selfless quest?
For its demands are unrelenting,
demand all of self,
even life itself.

Sacred Music and Inspiration

From that other world and other air
shared by beauty and by prayer;
from a higher, nobler, purer love
that lies beyond the earth, somewhere above;
a rhythm not yet heard
unfolding truth, the timeless Word.
Harmonies before unfelt that resonate within,
fire in the soul and all that's God therein;
matching the silence that they fill
and every other thought and passion still;
transforming, striking to the core
till God both heart and soul adore;
and every thought gives birth
to a love uniting heaven and earth.

Missionary of Charity

Watching her moving
between light and shadow,
amid the sick and dying,
her deft but gentle hands,
ordinary but extraordinary.
Grace lights her face,
tender compassion,
ministering love.

Seeking the world beyond
in quiet prayer,
prepared by silence
for the terror of God's beauty;
heart poured out
in tears of joy,
loving beyond thought
what is beyond thought.

Mary, Lily of the Valley

The Lily surprises,
soft-looking and beguiling
with her steely strength.
Petal power, perfume-scented punch
breaking through to shine.
Nothing can restrain her,
fulfilled in offering
her fragrant whiteness,
grateful for her gift of life.

Mary, fruitful virgin,
strong, determined,
challenging convention.
By God's power in her
great things are done,
her lowliness exalted.
Her song of gladness
sung for all of us,
grateful for her gift of life.

God's Love

The furrowed field.
Dark branches stark
against the winter sky,
trees untouched as yet
by the warming sun of spring.
But all is hid there,
waiting for the season to be ripe.

God's love as yet
seems hid.
But he is nearer
than we think,
nearer than each breath.
God's beauty waiting
for the season to be ripe.

Nothing Can Express

Nothing can express
God's tender love
outside of heaven above.
Nothing can express
the kiss of
the soul's inbreath at birth;
at death the kiss of
the soul's return.

On earth we long to learn
the words of heaven above,
the language of God's love,
to draw a breath
of that heavenly air.
It's here we learn to bear
his awesome loving presence there.

How Will We Respond?

How do we respond to Love
when He comes to us in flesh and blood?
When He comes to us in those we meet,
in those who don't belong,
or in those who have done us wrong?
When He comes to us in the midday heat?
When He comes in need on a crowded street,
when it's easy just to pass?
Would we witness with our blood
like the martyrs in the past?
Do we have the freedom to say yes,
freedom from fear and selfishness,
to say yes to God's love; or will we know
the bitter fruit of a final no?
Will we be ready, how will we respond
with love or vain conceit,
when He comes to us,
when at last we meet?

Not I, Lord?

Each of us has dipped
his hand into the dish,
inside of each
the one who would betray:
'Not I, Lord, surely not I?'
Yes, we would three times deny
and each of us has run away.

The line dividing evil from the good
runs through each of us: the upright wood
of the cross where He embraced each one
and died that each be called the Father's son.
Now we have our lives to learn
to forgive as God forgives,
to embrace Him in return.

Will You Be His?

Will you be his?
Reach out and touch,
he comes with gifts
for those who love him much.

It is ever thus,
even in our sin;
God thirsts for us
that we may thirst for him.

From the depths of God's desire,
even in our blindness,
there comes a love like fire,
its beauty and its brightness.

It is a grace,
fire and heat;
you cannot grasp the space
where two worlds meet.

Will We Be Him?

Will we be him? —
embrace all, as
he embraced us,
stretched out
upon the cross;
not just admire
but follow;
love with the love
he gave us,
willed us to share
when he embraced us
with his wounded
selfless love.
That is the cross
he gave us—
not to look
and turn away
but to give
ourselves away.
Will we take up
our cross, stretch out
to follow him?

Dark Night of Faith

In a night that carries
all the gloomy weight of sin,
wounded, out of tune with love,
there comes a God who heals,
who means to purify,
transform in darkness.
A God who comes in power,
in white-hot piercing light
to penetrate the dark.

He comes first hidden,
pure love that's felt as pain,
to find a space
where he can enter in,
to widen and to empty
and to fill,
to take us where he wills,
far beyond our grasp,
where only he can take us.

Relying on faith alone.
Now unseen, just carried by
his love, a total gift,
in the darkness
running like a silver thread.
Clinging in naked trust,
reduced to nothing, finding all,
loving knowledge of
a deeper truth.

Dark night of love,
bright darkness,
where sin and brokenness
are healed, transformed.
The heart poured out,
becoming tears of joy;
somehow the soul's dark music
changed, seeming now
in harmony with heaven.

Held there in his love,
stripped of every layer,
undoing all that's false,
now emptied of all but him,
enlarging us to fill us.
Furnace of fire, of total love,
desire and urgent longing.
All I long for, all my joy.
Oh the thrill, in him alone.

In the Desert of My Heart

With desire and inner fire,
with the mouth of my heart
I drank your words.
With the eye of my soul,
with love and awe
I sought your light,
your truth no ear has heard,
your wisdom only love knows,
flowing from your living spring.

My senses all enlivened
by the fragrance of your word,
you renewed, transformed me,
filled me with repentant tears,
my heart with joy and yearning.
You touched me,
set my heart on fire,
began to fill
my unfulfilled desire.

Transfiguration

Stunned, thrown to the ground,
on the high mountain close to God,
where Christ is seen in glory,
all shining brighter than the sun.
The apostles glimpsing
through the masking cloud,
encountering his otherness,
with joy now overcoming fear.
Rupture of time and space,
with Christ transfigured, uncreated light.

Explosive force of God's love
breaking through all barriers,
teaching truths, eternal mystery.
God's voice, 'listen to him',
transforming hearts to hear
Christ's message of the Cross
and the Resurrection yet to come.
Mere dress rehearsal
of the final drama, rising to
the fullness of his glory.

Christ teaching us the summit
of the love affair of prayer,
giving graces everywhere.
Garment of light
in which we're shrouded,
which we have clouded,
will once more be bright,
set others' hearts alight.
Sowing seeds to flower,
flooding hearts with fire.

Advent

Make space for the One
who is to come;
already come,
in faith awaited.
Prepare a place
to receive his grace.

Watch and pray,
in silence wait,
that on that joyful day
his true light will make
all that's dark depart,
when Christ comes to your heart.

Learn to have such hope and longing,
for Christ and his new coming,
that through you his love
will others touch,
if you but learn
to love him much.

Christmas Vigil

Mother of God,
with the Christ child
visit me this night.
As I watch in prayer
transform me,
birth me into God.

With the daybreak,
his Word upon my lips,
filled with his joy
and grace, transformed
to receive afresh
the Word made flesh.

Christmas Lectio

In the silence
of falling snow,
the Word comes
gently to my heart,
its beauty whispered
deep and hidden
before the dawn light,
its virgin presence
making all things new.

Why We Exist

Why we exist—
to accept the risk,
to lay down our guard,
all masks discard,
open up to change
for life to re-arrange,
mistrust for faith exchange.
It's gain not loss
to take up our cross
in faith and trust,
for Christ to appear in us.
Both joy and pain
are in the frame,
life's emptiness
and fullness,
while we learn to bear
the Father's love,
to answer
love with love.

What is Life For?

What is life for?—
if not to feed,
transform the soul,
become like God
who made us,
his Word written
on the heart,
to receive his love
poured out,
to turn from sin
and turn to him
in faith,
to do his work,
bring others
closer to him?

Who Am I?

Memory and imagination
tryst. If I am this—
past and present
momentarily uniting,
projecting snatches of my life
into my imagination,
so making progress
to the future:
then I am this—
thought patterns shed
and peeled away
to reveal a naked soul
alone, expressed
in mystery and longing.

Mathematics of the Heart

The night a living thing,
my heart sings,
hearing sharpened, every sense
in tense suspense.

Love flows through
early morning dark,
your words so true,
written on the heart.

With heart and soul in company,
our love a harmony
encircled by the stars,
mathematics of the heart.

The Caught Moon

Night comes softly
and the caught moon
shivers, trapped
in black branches.

Stars hang shining
like eyes in love,
as the silver wind
disturbs the stillness.

Black wings hover
as I shudder,
out alone, unknown
in the cold darkness.

Do Not Go Back

We caught the bus
to go back fifty years,
to find the old house
as it was,
that part of town unchanged
from cricket green
to railway line,
the school, the church
that I attended, served
Mass at seven; of course
the scale much larger
in my infant mind.

'Yes, all have died',
she said, but she remained,
had been there eighty years.
Inside it was as time stood still;
when all the world had changed
it had remained the same,
Edwardian décor, furniture and fittings,
at the house in the next street
I remembered visiting at seven.
As we said farewell,
I knew I would not return,
would not break the spell.

The taxi driver said,
'Yes, that part has stayed the same.'
We passed bright shops, boutiques,
new warehouse units,
clubs and blocks of flats.
He asked me where
the Fair Green had been
but all seemed foreign now.
It was strange to me
but I could see
it was I had changed.
I am not the same.

Fear of Losing You

The slim model
I had my eye on
is on my lap.
Silky bright thing
I can't keep my eyes off,
constantly watchful, alert,
waiting to respond
to its every signal.
I have such fear
of losing friends,
but the battery is low
and it is low on funds.

Then why not fall back
on the one true God,
who never fails us?
If we seek him,
we need have no fear
of losing friends;
he will give us all,
his love poured out upon us.
He knows all our needs.
He is always there for us,
watching, waiting,
always ready
to receive us.

Self Portrait

Practised hands
take up again
the once discarded canvas.
The palette knife repairs
beginner's brush strokes
painted thickly.
Youth's rawness
and aggressive style
softened now with age;
a subtler brush
reworks the portrait.
The garb remains,
off white and ivory black,
but the features and the pose
now loosened.

Warm colours
beginning to emerge,
cool colours
now receding.
Perhaps the chiaroscuro
will obscure, conceal,
the passing of the years;
but now there is a beauty,
a depth, a luminosity
contrivance cannot fake,
frank transparent
eyes that cannot hide
a peace and inner joy.
A face lit up by
a higher form of art.

Finding God in the Unexpected

Cutting through all that's not you,
through all that's limited and partial,
false and artificial,
to find you in the unexpected,
beyond all schemes and projects,
beyond the comfortable and neat,
all that once seemed full, complete.

Surprised by unhoped-for joy,
pure without alloy,
a love till then unknown;
seeking you alone,
the embrace of grace,
to find your face reflected in another,
herself professed your lover.

But seeking to possess,
to grasp and find you gone,
found lacking—
knowing now what you require,
love beyond this earth's desire.
Yet your glance, a touch enough
to hold me, set my heart on fire.

And as You Ask

And as you ask,
for love I took the risk.
Cut to the quick, the hurt
remained unhealed,
the issues unresolved,
all life's joys
now cast aside,
still torn inside
with loss and longing.

In dark despair
I turned to prayer.
Comfort comes, the grace
which comes with deep grief,
and something shifted
deep inside.
God does provide.
Now blessings flow
to risk again to grow.

Visited by Beauty

Visited now by beauty,
gently drawn to its embrace,
wounded by its kiss;
passion stirred,
disturbed by its effect,
unable to forget.
Tonight all things excite
remembrance of delight.
Taking a risk in total gift,
losing self in another self

to discover fullness,
recover oneness.
Love's encounter,
fire and heat,
thirst with thirst,
joy so intense unites
outside of self;
fullness of life
beyond this life,
life far beyond all limits.

Now Love Has Changed

Walking always together now,
together in the same direction,
the feeling different, somehow
the presence more intimate,
hidden in the everyday.
Love has changed,
different in every way

from when it was new,
wanting to meet, wanting
to admire, to hear,
face to face, to be near,
to visit every day.
Disappointed not to meet
again in the same way

now we are together,
always side by side,
discovering love is more,
discovering love is deeper,
no longer longing to look
just at each other, now looking
in the same direction.

Now You're Back

The Moon is high,
dusk has fallen,
the world has stopped,
the wind has dropped.
But now you're back,
making up for
all we've missed.

Moon on the water,
waves outrunning
the sadness.
Once more delight,
finding the way
through darkness
into light.

Along the Ridge

Between us
no word spoken
in the sunset's afterglow.
Winter stripped
down to zero
in the falling mist
along the ridge.
Stillness broken,
crows cawing,
echoing, re-echoing
in the bare trees.

Jade Sea

Silver sun and white rock,
jade sea stretching
to far blue mountains.
I walk miles of white sand
turning grey as night descends.
My thoughts distracted
by a fisher boat's lantern,
its fiery orange glow,
the slow lick of oar on water.

Silent Stillness

Walking mountain paths,
peak after peak,
stream after stream,
boundless, beyond thought.
Cold clarity, deep and still.
Beginning to feel the landscape.

Mapping the geography of the heart,
moving from the landscape of fear
to the landscape of love,
searching the contours
for the new and living way
that leads to life.

Solitude

Awakening to wilderness
Quiet mystery
Insight in the silver sun
Wisdom on the ocean's rim
Cliff top clarity
Sacred beauty awaits
A gaze, deep prayer
Thought and silence one